Passionate Purpose

Awakening the Inner Fire

A Little Workbook for
Life's Big Questions

Passionate Purpose

Awakening the Inner Fire

A Little Workbook for
Life's Big Questions

Reed F. Daugherity, M.C.

 **BookPartners, Inc.**
Wilsonville, Oregon

BookPartners, Inc.
P.O. Box 922
Wilsonville, Oregon 97070

Have you ever wondered:

"Why am I here?"

"Where am I going?"

"Can there be more to my life than this?"

"How can I impact the lives of others?"

These and many other questions are being asked by more people today than ever before. At the heart of these questions lies the most important question:

"What is my purpose?"

Table of Contents

How to Develop Your Life Purpose ... Twelve Steps to Finding Your Passion in Life

---

"Life is difficult," said M. Scott Peck in the first line of his book, *The Road Less Traveled.* The degree of difficulty seems enhanced when you are confronted by what appear to be small disasters: loss of a job, a devoted relationship gone bad, the feeling of malaise that comes with lack of purpose.

"Going inside" yourself for satisfying answers, for renewal of confidence is, perhaps, the best cure for vexing problems. But getting in contact with the inner voice, the source of infinite power that resides in each one of us is perplexing and frustrating for those who have not plumbed their depths with passion and insight. There is a four-line explanation that describes the confusion of the person who tries for the first or the hundredth time to define the central wisdom that resides within him:

- It's too close so we overlook it.
- It seems too good to be true so we can't believe it.
- It seems too profound so we can't fathom it.
- It's not outside ourselves so we can't obtain it anew.

For centuries, philosophers and mystics have taught that if you go inside you will find the fountain of wisdom. Statements like: "Liberate yourself and you liberate the world," have been pronounced by many teachers who interpret access to the spiritual center within each of us. "Open your heart, awaken your mind and you'll be there," is a popular instruction.

The problem is there are few adequate explanations of the process by which an individual can direct himself on the trip inward bound.

To that end this book has been written. It contains specific, practical, deep, probing, yet non-threatening questions to prepare and guide you on the journey inside.

The process outlined in this book is similar in fashion to *The Hero's Journey* described by Joseph Campbell:

"A hero ventures forth from the world of common day into a region of supernatural wonder; fabulous forces are there encountered and a decisive victory is won: The hero comes back from this mysterious adventure with the power to bestow boons on his fellow man."

As you start on the path of personal discovery you will become aware, as James Hillman declared in his book, *The Soul's Code:* "There is more in a human life than our theories of it allow."

"Sooner or later," Hillman continued, "something seems to call us onto a particular path. You may remember this 'something' as a signal moment in childhood when an urge out of nowhere, a fascination, a peculiar turn of events struck like an annunciation: 'This is what I must do, this is what I've got to have. This is who I am.'"

I hope this book will help to nudge you to probe your inner depths and to challenge you with the invitation it offers. And, perhaps, somewhere along the way you too, may declare: "This is what I must do, this is what I've got to have. This is who I am."

Most of us spend more than half of our lives earning a living. With our personal expenditures of time

---

having such value, it is vital that we address the issue of our "calling." As the French philosopher Albert Camus wrote: "Without work all life goes rotten. But when work is soulless, life stifles and dies. Like a hearty meal, soulful, enchanting, fun, meaningful work energizes and enhances our life to greater ends."

The following significant emotional events often demand from us the requirement that we investigate other realms of our lives:

Loss of a love

Tired, burned out

Death of a loved one

Loss of job

Bankruptcy

Lack of fulfillment, meaning, purpose

Spiritual separation

Feeling as if you have lost yourself within a relationship

Feeling possessed by another

Feeling lonely, alienated, depressed

Feeling imprisoned

Feeling "dead" inside

This book will help you identify areas in your life that are strengths from which to move forward.

After more than ten years of career and management consulting, I have identified one major "statement–question" that seems to spring forth from my clients as they consider where they are: "I wonder what I should do, now that I'm all grown up."

Most of them have made the comment with a dash of humor. However, underlying the humor there is dead seriousness in their voices. I have attempted over these years to help my clients solve that key question only to discover that the answer is much bigger than I had estimated. From these challenges I developed what I have called the "Path of Purpose."

Today, perhaps more than any other time in our social and economic history, we are challenged to find our purpose. We are thrown into confusion by vast technological changes and may feel as if we are hanging in thin air. No longer do we have constancy of work, permanence in living locations, and traditional belief systems. Change is rampant and will continue. The question to which, apprehensively, we already know the answer, is: Must we constantly grope for balance and cope without some reliable "steadiness" in our lives? The answer is seemingly yes. This "steadiness" we seek can be found in the "Path of Purpose." Living our lives on purpose. When we follow our path of purpose, that which we do will create joy, fun, delight, energy, enthusiasm, genuineness and authenticity.

Just as every flower in a garden has a coded DNA to be a rose, carnation, iris, or whatever, each one of us has been given a purpose. That purpose is encoded within us. It is up to us to find out what our purpose is.

Have you ever met someone who is inspired with his life, occupation, or hobbies? He is enthusiastic and has a sense of fulfillment. He cares about others and about his "work." His energy seems to bubble from deep within. His actions and responses are authentic, not superficial, nor is he "playing a role" or "wearing a mask." His words and actions are congruent. People like him are living their purpose.

Many words have been used to describe purpose. They are: mission, meaning, passion, vision, vocation, fullness, calling. Joseph Campbell said, "Follow your bliss." Immanual Kant said, "The human heart refuses to believe in a universe without a purpose." Kenneth Hildebrand remarked: "Strong lives are motivated by dynamic purposes; lesser ones exist on wishes and inclinations. The most glowing successes are but reflections on an inner fire."

An inner fire, bliss! These are vivid words; strong words which equate purpose with a spiritual quest. At our present level of human understanding we are seeking connection with something greater than ourselves. A definition of our purpose leads inexorably to connection with our spiritual identity ... to the deep personal inner fire.

Purpose cannot be simplified as a goal to be written down, then followed. It is not an intellectual process. It is about feelings, feelings so deep that they become passion, a burning desire for fulfillment. Purpose is about answering your calling. Benjamin Disraeli said, "The secret of success is constancy to purpose."

Fredrick Hudson said, "Purpose is an expression of your ultimate concerns, the sum of your yearnings for what you may become, or devote your life to becoming. Purpose is an inspiration for and provides meaning to our lives." Thomas A. Kempis observed, "Life without a purpose is a languid, drifting thing; every day we ought to review our purpose, saying to ourselves: This day let me make a sound beginning, for what we have hitherto done is naught." Begin we must, and continue the course.

We must begin to look deeply within ourselves to discover the true enjoyment of loving our lives and work, embracing that which fulfills us. If we find the purpose which anchors us, balances us, and provides a sense of fulfillment, then we can escape the confusion, stress and anxiety that are created by changes in the world. We can experience peace.

You may be working at a job you don't enjoy. In fact, one study reported that upwards of ninety percent of our work force is unhappy with their work. When you love what you do, you will be more successful, have greater joy and be more productive in every area of your life. I'm talking about fullness. Mother Teresa observed: "It's not how much we do but how much love we put in the action that we do." Put love in what you do and get fullness back.

Discovering the path of purpose for yourself is, as I have explained, an internal journey. To make the journey you must search inside yourself by way of quiet thought, meditation, and the gentle conquest of true inner silence. It is Lama Surya Das in his book *Eight Steps to Enlightenment, Awakening the Buddha Within,* who explains how true inner silence is the requirement that the searcher for his soul must satisfy to reach the inner sanctum of himself:

"True inner silence puts you in touch with the deeper dimensions of being and knowing — gnostic

- -

awareness and innate wisdom. Because it is impossible to express the inexpressible, the spiritual sound or song of silence is beyond words and concepts. Mere words are weak translations of what we really mean to say. Inner silence and emptiness can help provide easier access to universal mystery and primordial being, for almost anyone, without relying on foreign forms and arcane concepts.

"Silence is the threshold to the inner sanctum, the heart's sublime cave. Silence is the song of the heart, like love, a universal language, a natural melody open to anyone, even the tone deaf or religiously challenged. Try going out into the woods or sitting very near the ocean's waves. Look up at the bright stars at night; open your mind's inner ear and listen to the lovely song of silence. Here is the joy of contemplative sweetness. Follow this bliss."

For centuries we have been reminded that self-investigation and self-inventory are the only ways to discover the truth within ourselves. Your purpose is part of that truth, and each of us may participate in that truth if we choose.

This book provides you with twelve steps to finding your purpose ... that truly enjoyable expression of yourself ... your passion. Completion of these steps requires answering questions. By asking yourself questions you challenge yourself, reach a degree of self-discovery, and find answers for your life. Questions, courageous, deep, thought-provoking, sometimes uncomfortable questions, help move you beyond common comfort zones and help you bring forth what's been hidden deep in your core. It is Ranier Maria Rilke who beckons us so beautifully to partake in the question process of discovery:

"Be patient toward all that is unsolved in your heart and try to love the questions themselves like locked rooms or books that are written in a foreign tongue. Live the questions now. Perhaps you will then gradually, without noticing it, live your way some distant day into the answers."

Rilke is challenging us to "live in the question." We are to look for the "why's" and the "how's." We are to look "beyond" — with questions. Answers then come. We must search — by questioning. It is the greatest single method to uncover the seemingly unknown within. And, this is our personal responsibility. By fulfilling your life passion you can do what you love doing, be happier, live longer, and be more generously compensated.

Follow these steps closely. Journal, write, think deeply, and converse with yourself and possibly others who know you well. Upon completion of the twelve-step process, you will know yourself better and hopefully know your reason for being.

Search peacefully; do not push yourself. Ask for spiritual guidance. Allow the information to come from within. Be patient with yourself and the process. You are embarking upon the greatest journey of your life ... discovering the purpose you are to express as a human being.

Let yours be a peaceful and rewarding journey.

To believe your own thought, to believe that what is true for you in your private heart, is true for all men — that is genius. Speak your latent conviction, and it shall be the universal sense; for always the inmost in due time becomes the outmost....

Ralph Waldo Emerson

In response to the suggestions above, what are your thoughts and feelings as you begin?

What concerns do you have about your life at this time? What is it that is causing you to begin your search now?

For what reasons did you pick up this book? Or, why might someone have given it to you?

If you were to write your purpose now, how would it read?

Notes:

*In a word, each man is questioned by life;
and he can only answer to life by answering
for his own life; to life he can only respond
by being responsible.*

Viktor Frankl
Man's Search for Meaning

Suggested guidelines for using these steps:

1. Spend a significant amount of time thinking about the questions or statements. Listen to quiet, soft music as you reflect.

2. Ask for guidance and assistance … from your Higher Power, God, or other source you are spiritually allied with.

3. Spend quiet time, pray, meditate. Listen. Allow the answers to come to you. Don't demand. Allow.

4. Write your response to the questions. Writing crystallizes thought. However you choose to … write. Journal, make notes. Get your thoughts on paper. Write the first things that come to mind before the mind chatter. They will take on a different form and meaning when written down. You may not be able to answer each question immediately. And, you may not even choose to answer each question.

   The Artist's Way, written by Julia Cameron, reminds us, "Anyone who faithfully writes morning pages will be led to a connection with a source of wisdom within." This process is the same.

5.   Review your previous writings.

6.   Keep track of your dreams, daily thoughts and ideas. This material will become part of you. It will begin to show in your conversations.

7.   Discuss your process only with others who are supportive and respectful. Critical evaluation by others may hinder your progress.

8.   Schedule specific daily time for your process. Make this a "ritual of time" for yourself.

You may note many of the above eight points are a part of a personal readying process we call "centering." A particular method I recommend using for centering is one that Alexander Everett teaches in his book *Inward Bound.* The process consists of visualizing the colors of the rainbow (red, orange, yellow, green, blue, purple and violet). "The colors," says Alexander, "are psychological trigger devices...." Each color represents a specific "thought" to elicit a physical, mental or emotional reaction. The whole idea of centering is to quiet the mind so that you can get into contact with the spiritual center of yourself from which the power of the universe is reflected in each individual. Alexander's centering procedure is printed in the Chapter Eleven with his permission.

You are embarking upon a most important journey. Your purpose will give meaning and direction to your life. If you are not already expressing your purpose, your life will begin to change during this quest. Hang on! Many have discovered phenomenal changes in their lives as a result of searching for and discovering their life purpose.

1

What Do You Love To Do?

What would you do even if you were not paid to do it?

....

....

....

....

What do you like to do when others are not making demands on your time?

....

....

....

....

What do you like to do in your spare time?

What are you doing when you are feeling "in the flow" of life; what are you doing when you are fully involved, concentrated, and totally absorbed?

What do you want to do when you "have more time?"

Under what conditions do you feel the greatest serenity and happiness? What keeps these occasions from happening more frequently?

What creates a feeling of being in control of your life? When have you felt independent? Autonomous?

What energizes you?

What brings you joy? What feeds your soul?

What feeds you so you feel fullness?

What are your own questions?

Notes:

Trust thyself: every heart vibrates to that iron string.

Emerson, *Self Reliance*

Reminder: Chapter Eleven in this book describes a process of Centering, a method by which you can remove yourself from outward noises and sounds and from the clatter of the busy thinking brain. Such a method, with variations, has been used for centuries by mystics and by ordinary seekers like you and me to get to the quiet center of ourselves, that place of superb welcoming silence which Lama Surya Das speaks of as the destination he sought:

"I have been fortunate enough to be able to visit most of the great temples of man, study in India and Tibet, and circle the globe several times in search of what I was looking for. Now I say what others have said: That one has seen nothing until one has come face to face with himself. Then each and every moment hosts the ultimate miracle, wherever we are. Truth and love are in the palms of our hands. For when we are illumined, the whole universe is illumined."

I was living in Scottsdale, Arizona, with a friend, Roger, until I "got my feet under me" following a devastating divorce. One evening Roger came to me with paper and pencil. "How about listing your blessings?" he said. At that time I didn't feel like I had any. Little did I know.

Later, another friend, Murray, and I were driving back from lunch when he asked, "What are your goals?" I was silent, dumfounded, as I hadn't really thought about it. I was also afraid to admit it.

Lastly, Cheryl, a woman I was dating at the time, said to me one evening over dinner, "Why don't you do professionally what you've done as an amateur?" That question hit me profoundly hard. I had never stopped to think that I could do in my "work life" what I did for fun, or that I was good at.

From those three precious friends came profound wisdom which I look to quite often.

So, I suggest to you: Count your blessings. What are your personal assets, strengths, interests, abilities? What have you got going for you? The questions that follow are designed to help you confront yourself, help you decide your state of happiness.

What are your goals? What is out front of you to invite you forward?

What do you love to do?

2

What Parts of Your Present Job/Life Activities Do You Thoroughly Enjoy?

- -

Think back to why you took your present job or chose your present career. What were your likes or dislikes about this job when you took it?

_____

_____

_____

What are your present likes, the things which bring satisfaction to you on this job? (Or other jobs you have done.)

_____

_____

_____

What "payoffs" (internal, non-monetary benefits) are you receiving now? What skills, strengths, or qualities are you utilizing, and how do you feel when doing them?

Do you sometimes feel happy for no reason at all, or only when everything is going your way?

Does a beautiful view, a lovely melody, someone's good fortune, create happiness within you, or is happiness limited to the satisfaction of your personal goals/choices?

Do others experience joy as a result of your work?

What do you usually do when something you hoped for does not turn out?

What opportunities for action are you most attracted to? For what reason(s)?

Is your work smaller than your soul?

Mathew Fox refers to the "Great Work" of the universe as service to humanity. How does what you do connect with this "Great Work?"

What does your work "interfere with?"

What do you learn at work?

What are you doing to reinvent the profession in which you work?

What are your own questions?

Notes:

... if there is no bliss in our work, no passion or ecstasy, we have not yet found our work. We may have a job, but we do not yet have work.
                                                              Mathew Fox

----

3

What Do You Naturally Do Well?

- -

You have been given some natural abilities. What are they? (Lead, follow, draw, fly, think, teach, read, write, etc....)

....

....

....

What comes easily to you? It doesn't have to be career-related. That at which you excel gives clues to your purpose.

....

....

....

....

In what aspect(s) of your life are you completely self-sufficient?

What brings you satisfaction? Dissatisfaction?

What is your skill base? (Those skills you use most often and may be compensated for; or you may have been trained in these skills.)

What are your interests? Your wants? Your needs? Your desires?

_____

_____

_____

_____

_____

What are those things that give you the greatest joy? (Do not allow judgments or limitations in your thinking. Let your thoughts free-flow.) If you don't know, ask others for feedback. Pray. Meditate.

Remember: "But to each one is given the manifestation of the Spirit for the common good." (1Cor.7) Joseph Campbell said: "Follow your bliss ...." Remember?

_____

_____

_____

_____

_____

What are your own questions?

_____

_____

_____

_____

_____

Notes:

_____

_____

_____

_____

_____

_____

_____

But surely nothing can be said to work that stands between a man and the fullness of his being.

Dick Richards, *Artful Work*

While training soon-to-be-downsized employees within a large international firm in the mid-eighties, I was facilitating a series of workshops about how to re-employ one's self. During the workshop I asked participants to identify their accomplishments, what they had done over the last several years. A hand went up from one of the women who said, "I've never done anything, I'm just a secretary." Those are just the challenges I love.

During the next several minutes I discovered this secretary had become her boss's right-hand person and had created a management tool to track upwards of several hundred people coming into and out of their department during the downsizing. (Employees were funneling through this department either en-route to other jobs within the organization or to leave the company at a specific time.)

When she completed the creation of the management tool, she proceeded to hand it to her boss which prompted him to say to her, "Since you have created it, why don't you manage it?"

Over a period of eighteen months, she saved countless hours of time and energy accounting for people in a highly transient situation.

She thought she had never done anything. How many of us think of ourselves in the same negative way?

4

What Are Your Ten Greatest Successes to Date?

Everyone has had something he has done and is proud of. What is yours?

Your accomplishment needn't be of any certain size; it may be simple or complex. Have you improved, changed, developed, created, or built something?

_____

_____

_____

What have others complimented you for?

_____

_____

_____

What is it about each accomplishment that holds a measure of success?

If you were to represent your "self" by drawing a picture or series of pictures, what would you look like? If you were to label the picture(s) what would you write ... a value, quality, significance?

What disciplines have you lived your life around?

Under what circumstances does your courage wane?

Have you ever been involved in a grass-roots action? What did it accomplish?

What is your genius?

How do you feel about the answers? (Happy, sad, glad, angry, excited, scared, competent, confident, etc.)

What are your own questions?

Notes:

_____

_____

_____

_____

_____

_____

_____

_____

_____

_____

_____

_____

People travel to wonder at the height of mountains, and they pass by themselves without wondering.

St. Augustine

Some years ago I was traveling along the Washington and Oregon coast with a companion from Texas. She had just experienced a divorce and didn't know what she wanted to do with her life. I asked her to give herself some quiet time along the beaches.

One day I purposely went off to play golf leaving her with a full day of quiet space. Throughout our trip I had asked her to ponder some questions. I reminded her before I left for golf that she might wish to re-examine those questions while I was gone. When I returned, she had truly spent her day "inside" answering the questions. She went home to Houston two days later.

The result? She quit her job, started her own business, bought a home, and has never looked back since.

The value of quiet time is not fully realized until afterwards.

5

Do You Have a *Cause Célèbre?*

What are you strongly committed to, i.e., whales, environment, peace, nonviolence, teamwork, education, teaching, creativity…? What are you not committed to?

What do you feel passionate about?

_____

_____

_____

_____

What is it about your cause or passion which attracts you?

_____

_____

_____

_____

What stands in the way between you and your passion? What do you think you stand to lose by pursuing your passion?

_____

_____

_____

_____

_____

Which has determined the course of your life more, chance or necessity?

What are the underlying values in your commitments, i.e., education, nature, creativity, family, spirituality ...?

What is the central organizing principle of your 'self?' Fame, fortune, desire to be loved, to be feared, to be envied, to be thanked? Others?

What privileges of life do you most respect?

What is it you could not risk losing without losing your sense of self?

How do you feel about the answers?

What other thoughts occur?

Notes:

A human being is part of the whole, called by us the Universe, a part limited in time and space. He experiences himself, his thoughts, and feelings as something separated from the rest — a kind of optical delusion of his consciousness. This delusion is a kind of prison for us, restricting us to our personal desires and to affection for a few persons nearest to us.

Albert Einstein

6

What Are the Ten Most Important Lessons You Have Learned in Your Life?

Perhaps it is that nature "speaks" to you. Or,

Work has been more important than play. Or,

"I am totally responsible for myself; I choose to blame no one." Or,

"Relationships with others are more valuable than work."

What might they be for you?

_____

_____

_____

_____

_____

_____

What is most valued by you? (This does not need
to be related to your work.)

....

....

....

....

....

What have you learned that you want to pass on to
your children or grandchildren?

....

....

....

....

Do you have to keep striving to achieve more in
order to be happy?

....

....

....

What is challenging to you in your work or personal life?

What is really very important to you? Really!

Find ways to throw yourself into confusion. Then find your way out.

What is your philosophy of life?

Where has love been expressed in your life?

_____

_____

_____

How have you allowed yourself to be loved?

_____

_____

_____

How do you feel when answering these questions?

_____

_____

_____

What are your own questions?

_____

_____

_____

Notes:

_____

_____

_____

_____

_____

_____

_____

_____

_____

_____

_____

I looked on child rearing not only as a work of love and duty but as a profession that was fully as interesting and challenging as any honorable profession in the world, and one that demanded the best that I could bring to it.

Rose Kennedy

I had just completed six months developing a vision, purpose, and life plan with one of my coaching clients. She has been exploring how to develop her creativity, and make a living at it. She also had been investigating many questions and feelings over the previous months.

During a recent meeting with her she mentioned one beautiful discovery: "Isn't it odd that after all these years the things I return to are the things I loved in my childhood — music and flowers?"

7

Are There Some Issues or Perceived Problems That Have Occurred Repeatedly in Your Life?

What patterns or circumstances keep re-occurring? What seems to be continually happening in your life? These may be positive or negative, i.e., creativity, types of people, "failure," "happenings," separation, tragedy, addictions, successes. Does there seem to be a central theme to your life?

Have relationships continued to "come and go" in your life? What meaning is there to this?

What rules do you follow now that you would never break under any condition? Do these rules help develop a feeling of being constrained or more free?

How have your priorities changed in the last five years, ten years, twenty years?

We are all seeking permission in life. What do you seek permission for? And in what ways?

Try out some new settings for yourself: location(s), dress, jobs, titles. This is a way of "reframing" yourself. Do something different!

What are your feelings?

Notes:

_____

_____

_____

_____

_____

_____

_____

_____

_____

_____

_____

It is better to follow the voice inside and be at war with the whole world, than to follow the ways of the world and be at war with your deepest self.

Michael Pastore

8

What Do You Daydream About Doing?

This is one way in which your subconscious speaks to you and it is in the deep subconscious that your beliefs reside.

Remember being a little child? As you peered out the window, what captured your imagination?

_____

_____

_____

_____

Where do your thoughts go when you are bored?

_____

_____

_____

What do you dream about? Day and night dreams are essentially the same.

When and where do you feel the most courageous? The most powerful?

Recall a previous time when you felt successful. What factors contributed to it being so?

What are your own questions?

Notes:

I have no doubt whatever that most people live in a very restricted circle of their potential being. They make use of a very small portion of their possible consciousness. We all have reservoirs of life to draw upon, of which we do not dream.

William James

9

Imagine Writing Your Epitaph. What Do You Want to Be Remembered For?

What things (qualities, events, ideals, rules, attributes, etc.) will your life be incomplete without? These access the essence of your life.

_____

_____

_____

_____

Reflect upon your life from the "sunset" of your life. What is important to be remembered?

_____

_____

_____

_____

What would you do differently than you are doing now? What is keeping you from doing these now?

_____

_____

_____

_____

_____

_____

What do you tell yourself when you lie down to sleep after you turn the lights out?

_____

_____

_____

_____

_____

_____

How do you feel about addressing your mortality?

What are your own questions? Feelings?

Notes:

_____

_____

_____

_____

_____

_____

_____

_____

_____

_____

_____

_____

_____

We are all uniquely common, yet commonly unique.

Reed F. Daugherity

10

What Would You Do
If You Knew You Could Not Fail?

Abolish from your mind statements like: "I'd like to do it, but I know I could never succeed." What is it you *would* like to do?

What are those things you would do if...?

In what aspect(s) of your life do you feel most free: when you are alone, or with other people? When you work or when you have free time? Is the feeling of freedom due to the knowledge that you can do anything you want, or, to the knowledge that you are doing what you "must" do?

_____

_____

_____

_____

_____

_____

_____

When you have a decision to make, ask which option will take you closer to your life's purpose, e.g., "Will this be congruent with my life's purpose?"

_____

_____

_____

_____

Be willing to adapt and change, even at a moment's notice. Be responsive.

Remember wandering a wooded path? It moves in many different directions and there are many choices to make. Happiness is a continuous path, a journey. What path have you been walking?

....

....

....

Each morning upon rising do the things that relate to your heart. What are these things?

....

....

....

....

What are your own questions? Feelings?

....

....

....

....

Notes:

I have no way of knowing what results my actions will have.... My only sure reward is in my actions and not from them. The quality of my reward is in the depth of my response.

Hugh Prather

11

Go Within. Be Still. Be Quiet.
Ask. Listen. Listen Attentively to
Your Internal Voice.

Your purpose is within you; each cell and fiber of your body responds and resonates to that purpose when it is put into action.

Your challenge is to listen to what your body wants to respond to. Listen to what you truly believe, deeply believe. What is anchored in your "being?"

Intuition is speaking … it is the guidance you have asked for. Listen. What are those thoughts you have put aside?

What have you been ignoring that has been tugging at your heart?

Of course, it is the inspiration and commitment you need to honor for the rest of your life.

What are those questions that come to you when you truly listen?

Monitor your feelings each day. What are your feelings today?

Notes:

_____

_____

_____

_____

_____

_____

_____

_____

_____

_____

_____

_____

Freedom consists not in refusing to recognize anything above us, but in respecting something which is above us; for by respecting it, we raise ourselves to it, and by our very acknowledgment, prove that we bear within ourselves what is higher, and are worthy to be on a level with it.

Goethe

In the very early eighties, my family was living in Calgary, Alberta, Canada. I had been employed as a vice president in a local oil company. I didn't particularly enjoy the work as I had no training in reservoir or geological engineering. My training had been as a pilot in the United States Air Force. My interests were far from the oil industry. However, the opportunities were great to expand my horizons and learning.

The oil company was sold four years after I arrived on the scene. Shortly thereafter I began my own venture into building commercial real estate. After spending two years with a stream of meetings and spending immense amounts of money, I thought I was impressing others and even myself until one day.

That was the day when I awakened with a gnawing in my stomach. It would not go away. The only thing I knew was that I wasn't happy. However, seemingly I had done all the right "things:" degree, military service, insurance for my family, education for my children in the "right" schools, and idyllic setting in which to live. I couldn't possibly be unhappy. I didn't even know how to say it.

As it turned out we moved to San Diego. Shortly thereafter, I was faced with a divorce and wondered

----

what to do with my changed life. After moving to Arizona and completing my graduate degree, I eventually discovered the "gnawing" was telling me to get my life on course. That's when I began the search for my own purpose.

Earlier, I wrote that centering is a practice by which the individual on the road to defining purpose in his life can reach inside himself to contact with the inner divinity. I also mentioned that I would introduce you to Alexander Everett, author of *Inward Bound,* the inspired teacher who was described in the early seventies as the man who was responsible for inspiring the human potential movement in the United States.

It is Everett who has graciously given his permission for me to reproduce here the centering procedure which he teaches to persons who attend his seminar Inward Bound, the name of which is the same as his book.

"When we center ourselves," says Alexander, "we introduce into ourselves several direct benefits as a result of aligning the body with the spirit."

Alexander Everett advises that centering should become a habit.

"We all need to center every day for at least fifteen minutes. If we do just fifteen minutes per day, the balance of the twenty-four hours will be much more in harmony. The best time to center is early in the morning. Perhaps you like to do your chores first — tend to the cat and dog, brush your teeth and so forth — or perhaps you like to center when you first get out of bed. Create your own magic."

According to Alexander, when a white light passes through a prism, the seven colors of the rainbow are formed. The lowest part is the color red, located on the outermost band of the rainbow. The highest is violet, the innermost color. So we go from red to violet to reach our innermost part of being. Red represents the physical part, the external. The next color, orange, is the emotional part, the color expressing feeling. Yellow symbolizes the mental. The fourth color is green, the color of peace. In order to reach the green peaceful state, you have to quiet the red physical part of you, calm the orange emotional part, and still the yellow mental part so that you can enter the fourth spiritual state.

The fifth color is blue, which represents love. Purple is the mental level of spirituality—the knowing level of the masters. Violet represents the spiritual-spiritual, where consciousness becomes one with God.

All of the colors, Alexander explained, are psychological trigger devices, a method to bring the individual peace by centering himself. Centering is not the only method of coming to peace, of course. It is the one Alexander uses, "because I wanted to find something that did not clash with Buddhism, Hinduism, Christianity, Judaism or any religion. Every religion will accept the colors of the rainbow. Every religion will accept nature. I have tried to create a universal spiritual language."

The Centering Procedure

Now, you can begin the actual steps of centering yourself. You start with the color red and progress, as you move deeper into yourself, to the color violet.

Following is an explanation Alexander Everett has written to take you step by step inward bound:

First, close your eyes and visualize the seven colors of the rainbow. You might wish to create a rainbow in your mind's eye and imagine yourself passing from the outside band of red inward toward violet. Slowly, as if you were a traveler on a quiet journey of self-discovery, pass through red, orange,

Go Within. Be Still. Be Quiet. Ask. Listen.   - 77 -

Listen Attentively to Your Internal Voice.

yellow, green. Depending on your visualization powers, you may actually see the different colors vividly as you progress through the rainbow stages. Your passage should be slow and silent, free of mind clatter and interruptions. Start your centering exercise by saying to yourself:

I now prepare to center myself. The first color I will visualize is red. I will actually see the color red in my mind, and in sequence as I progress, I will visualize the other colors of the rainbow.

Red:

I first will visualize the color red. I relax my body from head to foot. I relax, let go of my body. Relax.

When you release the muscles around the eyes, the throat area and the lungs, the rest of the body will let go.

Orange:

I next visualize the color orange. I release and let go of all of my emotions. I desire only that which is good for others.

To forget yourself and your desires, direct your energy into the desire to help others. Put aside your own desires and say,

>*I want to help my fellow man the best way I can.*

When you do this your personal desires and needs become less.

Yellow:

>*I calm and still my mind, I bring my mind to rest.*

This is the statement you say to yourself. To still the mind, see yourself somewhere in nature — in a park, by a river, in the desert, in a garden — wherever it is natural for you to be. When the mind is surrounded by nature, your thinking slows down, you become more peaceful.

Green:

>*I allow peace to come into my life. I sense a state of peacefulness within every cell of my body.*

Now you can enter peace: you have stilled your body, stilled the emotions and stilled the mind.

Blue:

>*I let love permeate my entire being. I feel myself full of love.*

Many people cannot love because they are not at peace. How can you love when you are upset mentally, physically and emotionally? Peace comes before love.

Purple:

I seek out the depths within. I aspire to that inner secret place.

Purple is the master level of accepting and knowing who you are. When you are peaceful and loving, you then desire the very highest, you aspire to that which is beyond.

Violet:

I enter the inner-most part of my being. I am now there. I am centered.

The whole purpose of life is to know who you are, that you are of God and to return to that knowledge. And you can do it by following the seven steps of the rainbow. You do this by releasing your body, releasing your emotions, and releasing your mind; entering a peaceful state, loving of others, desiring oneness with God. This is a natural sequence; you become centered.

In the last stage of being centered you say to yourself:

I am now one with my inner-self, a state which encompasses all of time, so that I just become aware of the totality of the now. I am only conscious of the present. I feel and sense this one moment in time ... I just realize myself right now.

We live in a three dimensional world that tells us there is yesterday, today and tomorrow. But when we are centered, we enter the spiritual realm and the only time is now. Reality is that there is no yesterday and there is no tomorrow. There is only the now.

12

How Is It You Want to Serve Others?

- -

True purpose is about service — serving others. In what way(s) are you to serve humanity?

Are you comfortable with the thought that the shape of the future and humanity depends on how you invest your energy now? What consequences do you draw from this?

Given what you have learned and consequently now know about yourself, what makes you happy; what are the freedoms and constraints of your life, what do you think you can contribute to the making of history? And what would be the consequences if you did nothing?

_____

_____

_____

_____

_____

_____

_____

_____

_____

_____

_____

_____

_____

What are your own questions?

Notes:

I don't know what your destiny will be; but one thing I know: The only ones among you who will be truly happy are those who have sought and found how to serve.

Albert Schweitzer

13

What to Do with Your Answers

First and foremost, do not judge your writing or yourself. Celebrate your process and progress. It takes courage. You have entered a dialogue with self. This is holy, sacred ground, ground where new life can be born. Trust in the possibility of a newness here. The process you have begun never ends, for you are on the wisdom path. Divine wisdom often enters through the windows of irrelevance. You may now or very soon in the future be living a life you have never lived before. What is crucial is often hidden. It takes courage to face what has not been lived before.

There is a mystery at work here. There is a place, a knowing, an understanding available to each of us. Let this process sink into that mystery. Embrace it. Allow it to grow, develop. The warmth of your embrace will give it birth. Be available for the mystery to whisper to you from the silence. In the words of Clark Moustakas:

"Mystery speaks to me in tacit ways, whispering secrets of life and death, pointing to vague and ambiguous possibilities, largely unrevealed. No further probing is helpful, yet strangely, unexpectedly, in a covenant with silence a striking transformation occurs. Without explanation, the darkness turns to light; hopelessness points the way to courage; life takes on a new determination. A door opens again; the path is inviting; intimate signs light up along the way.

"Mystery offers an opportunity for change: it induces unknown powers at work within us and in the world, forces that turn the impossible dream toward glimmerings within the self; an inward key unlocks the prison and brings a renewal of hope, often only in fragments at first, but ultimately everything is connected and in harmony once more.

"Out of the darkness and the mystery that leads to self-renewal, the miracle of growth occurs again. I am inspired to return to life with others. They talk to me or sit in silence. I listen or speak. We create new perspectives, new awarenesses and understandings. The illumi-

----

nating shift occurs because we have revealed ourselves to each other. We have disclosed the secrets of our world. We have encountered the mystery of I and Thou, in words and silences in the spaces in between, in deep-down places, in inward churnings, in tacit ways and internal rhythms, in universal powers that transport us to new realizations of each other and the life we share."

Hopefully, by the time you finish the question process printed in this book, the answers will be evident. Should they not be, perhaps further investigation is necessary. You may need to develop further questions or return to some of your earlier questions and answers.

Sit with your process and answers for awhile. Let the information distill and "gel." Patience is the distillate here. Ask yourself how you feel about what has come for you: "What is it that I do next?" Also, how might you feel about not knowing?

If you are working professionally with someone such as a counselor, psychologist, coach, mentor, or just a friend, share what you have learned. By speaking your answers you will further develop your knowing of the information. It will help you determine if the information "rings true." The internal process comes with no guarantees. Yet, it is the only guaranteed process, whatever time

----

it takes. And, in the process there is no guarantee that it won't change in the future. Change is the nature of things, always has been, and always will be. You may complete the process and decide to change it. Take responsibility for it and do it from a more empowered and informed position. You have the power to choose your next step. Do it. Do it while being more informed and with feeling. Make your own recovery the first priority of your life. Give yourself permission to begin, to be a beginner — all over again if need be. Celebrate this process for yourself. Many others have never taken the steps you have taken, or are about to take.

The information you develop through this process will, in all probability, enlighten at least one small step. Take it. The rest will be made known to you. Here patience and trust are your allies along the path of discovery.

Lastly, gather support for yourself and your process. Seek others who are now on the discovery path and talk with them. Share your information. You may discover many others are feeling similar to you, and the process you have just gone through can be helpful to them.

Now that you have finished your personal investigation, you are ready to bring all your thoughts, feelings and other information together. For some, the process illuminates their purpose and no further work may be necessary. For others, organizing their information is necessary to be able to proceed. Questions, once again, serve our process. From all you have gathered, what do you now believe to be your personal uniqueness? What is it about you that is different? It may be a combination of qualities, strengths, abilities, characteristics. Define your uniqueness in a short statement of twenty-five to fifty words.

Vision

Once you have a clear picture of your uniqueness as a human being you next create your vision. Your vision is a statement about who you are, the essence of your being. It is your highest ideal, the highest truth of your being. Your vision is a consistently held mental image of a possible reality.

It may be helpful to go back over your written material and glean the key words that stick out and speak to you about you. Identify those words that draw feeling from within you as you read them, that "ring a bell," or resonate deeply. From those words begin to shape them together into a statement of who you are. That is your vision.

Begin your vision statement with "I am...."

Purpose

Now you are ready to create the actual "thing" you will do to fulfill your vision. What is it you are going to do to bring forth your vision for your life?

What actions will you take to realize your vision? Another way to understand your vision is to see yourself, as I suggested earlier, at the sunset of your life looking back. If you could change your life, how would you draw a new path?

You may want to begin your purpose statement with: "To serve, to provide, to assist." Make it an action statement.

You may now want to create a strategic plan with choices and goals to carry out your vision and purpose. Make your choices and goals specific, time-dated actions which need to be accomplished to fulfill your purpose.

As you work on your purpose and vision, you should realize how consciousness of the world has changed. Today, most of us have not learned to look deeply for internal guidance. We have learned to focus on short-term goals. A journey I made to Peru may give you an insight to lofty but practical heights developed by a remarkable people.

The Inca culture was the subject of our trip to Peru. We noted the grand and intricate stone architecture, highly developed farming and terracing systems and integration of the work of these peoples, their social lives, and the religious / spiritual aspects of their lives as part of their whole culture.

What impressed me were the stones (boulders from 50 pounds to 350 tons) cut precisely and fitted together so well that water would not flow between them and earthquakes couldn't move them out of place. The farm terracing of this ancient culture produced three to four times the amount per liter of water than did the valley floor below. They experimented with seeds at precise altitudes for optimal growth. They created delicate planned communities which protected themselves from the elements and their enemies. They revered nature's beauty, and their own. Every aspect of their lives, work, politics and spiritual pursuits were very tightly woven together.

     As our group attempted to experience the 400- to
500-year-old culture through meditation, conversa-
tion, and standing awestruck in the presence of such
inexplicable grandeur, it became very obvious to me
that these vanished people had a profound sense of
vision and purpose. They knew who they were — a
people of great spiritual wealth, connected very
closely to the earth and its energy. Their purpose?
Every detail, from ritual baths draining into lucrative
farming fields, cutting stones along sensitive
"weaker" lines (every stone had a "purpose"), imple-
mentation of astronomy for specific dates to plant,
and planned cities depicting their reverence for the
earth and the water it provided, demonstrated their
sense of purpose.

     I was touched more than once by the "energy" of
peace, serenity, and power in the ancient cities. The
inhabitants seemed to understand how to do things we
only dream about. In one case, an eighty-ton carved
stone had been left along a roadway just short of its
destination. Four hundred fifty years earlier, it had been
cut to put into its precise place and dragged (?) from its
quarry 2,000 feet above the site where we found it over
four miles away across the valley floor and through a

----

powerful river. I scratched my head in wonder as to how they might have done this.

It seemed every move they made was one with a "knowing" planned sequence as part of an intricate, intimate dance in which all worked and lived. To me this indicated vision, purpose, commitment, and personal power.

What is your eighty-ton stone — and your vision and purpose behind it?

I hope you have discovered that purpose is much larger than goals. It is a much greater sense of internal force. It relates to your basic belief system, your values. Purpose is inner work, as you have discovered. This inner work is constantly necessary in our lives to keep us on course or on our "Path of Purpose." And, it is possible to change our purpose through our life. According to Fredrick Hudson: "Purpose is a profound commitment to a compelling expectation for this time in your life. No one has the same sense of purpose throughout an entire life." We may have a different sense of purpose at different ages and stages as our values change and vary, but what doesn't change is the power of discovery which is released when we delve within ourselves to find who we are.

For most, the development of purpose is not easily accomplished. It requires a disciplined approach, as you may have experienced. The more you look to purpose in everything you do, the more you relate to it. Continue asking yourself in everything you do, "What is the purpose behind what I am doing?" Your personal vision and purpose will continue to guide you.

For those of you who are associated with organizations, you may find this process and some of these specific questions helpful. To find organizational purpose, meaning, direction, vision, and in turn profitability and creativity, the process is much the same.

I hope this has been a wonderful and fruitful journey. The wisdom of the sages tells us we have only just begun. Staying on your path of purpose is a great challenge of life. However, if you are following your purpose you are experiencing the joy of the journey.

I wish you peace and joy in expressing your purpose.

Each man has his own vocation. The talent is the call. There is one direction in which all space is open to him ... Anything man can do may be divinely done.

Emerson, *Spiritual Laws*

References

Cameron, Julia. *The Artist's Way.* Los Angeles, Jeremy P. Tarcher/Perigee, 1992.

Campbell, Joseph, Stuart L. Brown and Phil Cousineau. *The Hero's Journey: The World of Joseph Campbell.* San Francisco, Harper and Rowe, 1990.

Cowan, John. *Small Decencies, Reflections and Meditations on Being Human at Work.* New York, HarperCollins, 1992.

Czikszentmihalyi, Mihaly. *Flow: The Psychology of Optimal Experience.* New York, HarperPerennial, 1991.

Czikszentmihalyi, Mihaly. *The Evolving Self: A Psychology for the Third Millennium.* New York, HarperCollins, 1993.

Everett, Alexander. *Inward Bound,* Wilsonville, OR, BookPartners, 1998.

Fox, Mathew. *The Reinvention of Work: A New Vision of Livelihood for Our Time.* San Francisco, Harper San Francisco, 1994.

Hillman, James. *The Soul's Code.* New York, Random House, 1996.

Hudson, Frederic M. and McLean, Pamela D. *Life Launch.* Santa Barbara, Self Published, 1993.

Lama Surya Das. *Awakening the Buddha Within: Eight Steps to Enlightenment.* New York, Broadway/ Bantam Books, 1997.

Moustakas, Clark. *Being–In, Being–For, Being–With.* Northdale, NJ, Jason Aronson, Inc., 1995.

Parry, Danaan. *Warriors of The Heart.* Cooperstown, NY, Sunstone Publications, 1994.

Richards, M.C. *Centering: In Pottery, Poetry, and the Person.* Middletown, CT, Wesleyan University Press, 1989.

Rilke, Ranier Marie. *Letters to a Young Poet.* Translated by Stephen Mitchell. New York, Random House, 1984.

Sinetar, Marsha. *Do What You Love, The Money Will Follow.* Paulist Press, 1987.

Start by doing what is necessary; then do what is possible; and suddenly you will be doing the impossible.

St. Francis of Assisi

This is the true joy in life,

the being used for a purpose
recognized by yourself as a mighty
one;

the being thoroughly worn out
before you are thrown on the scrap
heap;

the being a force of Nature
instead of a feverish selfish little clod
of ailments and grievances
complaining that the world will not
devote itself to making you happy.

George Bernard Shaw

About the Author

Reed Daugherity is currently an organizational consultant and certified professional and personal coach located in Spokane, Washington.

He counsels and consults to individuals and organizations undergoing change and transition in their lives and systems. Reed assists corporations in their transformation to a consciousness of mastery and success. His primary focus is coaching, outplacement, and facilitating vision and change in organizations and individuals.

Reed holds a Master of Counseling degree from Arizona State University, has been an MBA faculty member at Western International University in Phoenix and is presently an adjunct faculty with Eastern Washington University, and Western Washington University. He is also a member of National Speakers Association and the Professional and Personal Coaches Association.

Reed invites your comments regarding your discovery process. He can be reached at:

509-623-9717

e-mail reedcoach@aol.com

All men should strive to learn before they die
What they are running from, and to, and
why.

James Thurber

Go confidently in the direction of your
dreams.

Live the life you've imagined. As you
simplify your life, the laws of the universe will be
simpler.

Thoreau